# An Introduction To Freemasonry

## What is it and how to join?

## By Ray Fox

First Edition published in 2016 by The Bottom Line Consultancy

Hurst Cottage, Bottle Square Lane, Radnage,

Buckinghamshire. HP14 4DP, United Kingdom

Tel: 01494 483728 Fax: 01494 484039

Email: fox@estelle-alan.com

ISBN-13: 978-1533439062

ISBN-10: 1533439060

First edition 2016

Printed and bound by Amazon Creates

NOTE: The material contained in this book is set out in good faith for general
guidance and no liability can be accepted for loss or expense incurred as a result of
relying in particular circumstances on statements made in this book. Laws and
regulations are complex and liable to change, and readers should check the current
positions with the relevant authorities in their country of origin before making
personal arrangements.

This book is available online and at all good bookstores.

# Contents Page

# Introduction

If you asked one hundred Freemasons why they went to Masonic meetings, you'd probably get a hundred different answers. If you analysed further and pressed them to give you a more detailed response, you'd probably get the same answer – they enjoy it. But each one of those hundred Freemasons probably enjoy different aspects of Freemasonry. Freemasonry means different things to different people.

I have often thought of Freemasonry as being like a smorgasbord – different people pick and choose different aspects of Freemasonry that gives them pleasure. It follows that whatever it is that they enjoy doing within the Masonic sphere, they feel that they want to come back for more and because they enjoy it, they want to introduce their friends and family to Freemasonry as well.

The difficult aspect of all this is that if you're interested in becoming a Freemason, it's pretty confusing if you want to get some simple insight into exactly what Freemasonry is all about and what BEING a Freemason actually involves.

To take an analogy, if you were interested in joining a chess club, you'd know that once you become a member, you'd play chess. The same goes for, say, joining a bridge club, a golf club or a salsa dancing club.

With Freemasonry, it's completely different. Although there is information that you can glean from various web sites, until you actually become a member and join a Lodge, you really have no idea what being a Freemason is all about.

This book gives the prospective candidate [someone who wants to join a Masonic Lodge] a brief introduction and overview of Freemasonry, what goes on at meetings of a Masonic Lodge and what happens at the meal after the meeting – known as *The Festive Board.*

There are quite literally tens of thousands of books written about Freemasonry.  There are hundreds of Masonic libraries with huge tomes which analyse and explain every tiny detail of what Freemasonry is about, its history, its members, etc.

That is NOT what I am trying to do.  I have been involved in Freemasonry for over 35 years.  I have Senior London Grand Rank in Craft Masonry, I have London Grand Chapter Rank in Royal Arch and Provincial Grand Ranks in Mark Masonry and The Order of the Secret Monitor.  What I have written here are my own views, experiences and opinions of Freemasonry.

I have neither sought nor obtained approval from The United Grand Lodge of England [UGLE] for permission to write this book although I doubt that my views and opinions are in any way at variance with those of UGLE.

Likewise, this book is not in any way a negative exposé of Freemasonry.  My hope, once you have read this book, is to feel sufficiently confident about approaching your local Masonic lodge or province and talking to them about the possibility of joining.

Equally, I'd like to think that new Freemasons, and of course their partners, come to appreciate the very real benefits of becoming a Freemason, not only for themselves but also for the community.

I should emphasise that I know nothing about Womens' Freemasonry. Likewise, Freemasonry in Scotland and Ireland have different jurisdictions.

UGLE oversee Freemasonry in England and Wales and links to the websites for all these bodies are given at the end of the book.

# How I first got interested in Freemasonry

I can't honestly say that I was looking to join Freemasonry. It sort of crept up on me. In the early 1980s, I was the Assistant Company Secretary of an East London Lift Engineering Company.

I had qualified as a Chartered Secretary and The Institute of Chartered Secretaries used to produce an annual hand-book of activities involving the Institute.

The hand-book mentioned people who had qualified, the jobs members had achieved, the various charities that were being supported and the various sub groups that the institute was involved with.

There was a golf club, a church group, a choir group plus various other social and business activities.

One of the groups mentioned was the "Semper Vigilans Masonic Lodge". Semper Vigilans was the institute's motto – it was the Latin for "always vigilant".

All it said was that the "Semper Vigilans Masonic Lodge met in Holborn and that new members were always welcome. A phone number was included.

I have since learned that you have to be at least 21 years old to join but there is no upper age limit. In one of the lodges that I am associated with, the Master was 98 years old when he became Master. Many men find they have time on their hands as they get older, especially as they approach retirement and so it's not unusual for men in their 60s to join. On the other hand, there are a number of University schemes to encourage younger men to join.

I had never heard of Freemasonry and I had no way of finding out what it was all about.

For some of the younger readers, this might be hard to envisage but this was before email, before the internet and long before search engines had ever been invented.

So I called the number and asked the person at the other end of the phone if he could tell me what was involved. His terse reply was "No". I then asked him if he could send me some information. The response again was "No".

I then said to him that if he couldn't or wouldn't tell me anything over the phone and likewise couldn't or wouldn't pop anything in the post to me, how was I going to consider whether this was something I wanted to get involved with or not.

He took my phone number and promised to pass it on to someone who would make contact.

Two weeks later, I got a phone call from someone who told me that he was a Past Master of Semper Vigilans Masonic Lodge [not that I actually knew what a Past Master was at that time] and we arranged to meet at a coffee shop on the concourse of Liverpool Street station the following week.

He duly turned up with another member of the lodge who he introduced as one of the deacons in the lodge.

Mr. Past Master told me that he was also the Past Master of another lodge that met in London. When I asked him what was the benefit of joining two different Masonic lodges, he gave me his stock reply, which was "when you join, you'll understand why".

I was with Mr. Past Master and Mr. Deacon for about two hours in all. I asked them what I considered to be a number of reasonably intelligent questions and I got virtually the same reply to each question: "when you join, you'll understand why".

After two hours, our meeting came to a natural conclusion. Mr. Past Master asked me if I was interested in joining.

I told him that I'd like to do some research and find out a bit more about Freemasonry to which he told me that even if I wanted to join, I couldn't join anyway. I was confused so I asked him why I couldn't join. He told me that he and Mr. Deacon had to have known me for a minimum of six months before they could put my name forward to the Lodge Committee for interview.

So that was where it was left.  They would contact me in six months' time to see if I was interested in progressing my membership.

Quite frankly, I quickly forgot all about Freemasonry and got on with the rest of my life.

Six months later I got a call from Mr. Past Master.  He wanted to know whether I'd like to meet with him and Mr. Deacon again to progress possible membership.

We met again but this time I was better prepared.  I had written out a list of twenty questions to which I wanted specific answers to before I would consider joining.

I was disappointed to receive virtually the same answer to every question that I asked - "when you join, you'll understand why".

After another two hours of them avoiding answering any question that I asked, I decided I'd had enough and decided to leave.

They asked me if I was interested in joining and I told them that I wasn't. "Why?" they asked.

I told them that they wanted me to spend a lot of money to join an organisation that I couldn't find anything out about, I was expected to donate money to charity but I don't know who the beneficiaries are, I have to swear an oath of secrecy on the bible but I can't read the wording in advance and I have absolutely no idea what goes on at the meetings anyway, to which I was told again: "when you join, you'll understand why".

So I went home and didn't give Freemasonry another thought until a few weeks later when Mr. Past Master called me again.

He invited me to a gathering being held in London in a couple of weeks' time which he called "an LOI supper". He never explained to me what an *LOI* was but I have since discovered it stands for *Lodge of Instruction*. He told me there would be a number of other lodge members there as well as a number of non-masonic guests, some of whom were also considering joining the lodge.

I thought it would be a bit churlish of me not to go so I decided to go along and see what happened.

Actually, very little happened. Neither Mr. Past Master nor Mr. Deacon turned up. Hardly anybody spoke to me, I had no idea who were lodge members and who were guests and I thought that the sooner I went home the better.

After about 15 minutes, we were asked to take our seats for dinner.

There was a top table where what I thought were the dignitaries sat and there were three branches coming off from the top table, like a large letter "E".

The gentleman in the centre of the top table who was called The President, welcomed everybody.   There was someone they called The Chaplain who said a few words as "grace before meals" and there was a toast to the Queen, but they were only formalities.

I didn't know who were lodge members and who were guests so I turned to the gentleman sitting next to me. I introduced myself to him and we started chatting.  I asked him what he did for a living.  He told me that he had one of the greatest jobs in the world.

I was intrigued.  What could possibly be one of the greatest jobs in the world?  He told me he was in the army.   Much as I respect members of the armed forces, I still couldn't relate to this being the greatest job in the world.  He told me he was in the Cavalry. This intrigued me even more.  Did we STILL have Cavalry?

He asked me if I had ever seen "The Trooping of The Colours" or the ceremony of firing the guns in St. James's Park on the Queen's birthday? Of course I had.

So he told me that he was a Captain in the Cavalry.  He was one of the guys who rode one of the black horses that pulled the carriage and fired the guns in St. James's Park on the Queen's birthday.

I was fascinated and I asked him dozens of questions about his life in the Cavalry.

To be honest, I couldn't get this guy out of my mind.  I had just had dinner with one of the guys who rode one of the black horses that pulled the carriage and fired the guns in St. James's Park on the Queen's birthday.

My life was pretty dull compared to his. I spent my time handling legal documents, reading contracts and leases, running my employer's pension plan and sorting out insurance claims.

The thought kept coming back to me over and over again. Doing what I do, where would I meet someone as unusual as him?

So I called Mr. Past Master and told him that I had decided to join.

By pure fluke, it was one of the best decisions I have ever made.

The irony is that I never met the man from the Cavalry again. I never knew his name, I have no idea whether he was a member of a lodge but unbeknown to him, he was the reason why I decided to join a lodge.

Over the years, I have met quite literally dozens and dozens of incredible and fascinating people. I have met two British Ambassadors, an airline pilot, a fighter pilot in the present day air-force, a World War Two bomber pilot who flew Lancasters during the war, a captain of an oil tanker, a forensic pathologist, one of Tony Blair's bodyguards when he was prime minister, a chairman of an international charity, someone who was involved in identifying bodies of people who were drowned in the Tsunami in Indonesia, a store detective, a Commander in the Navy who specialises in oceanography, a businessman who imports railway sleepers into the UK plus dozens of Solicitors, barristers, accountants, actuaries, company directors, architects, surveyors, politicians, etc. I have also met builders, plumbers, postmen, electricians, etc.

In the weeks prior to writing this, I have met a retired maths teacher, someone who repairs and services grandfather clocks, a farmer who specialises in dairy farming and a BT engineer who specialises in internet installations.

All of this was due to me meeting one of the guys who rode one of the black horses that pulled the carriage and fired the guns in St. James's Park on the Queen's birthday.

# History of Freemasonry

Freemasonry is without a doubt the oldest fraternal association in the world. Over the years its members have included Kings, Dukes, American Presidents, Prime Ministers, Admirals, Judges, Politicians, Opera Stars, Sportsmen, Movie Stars, etc. However, it has also welcomed as members Plumbers, Milkmen, Electricians, Salesmen, Lift Engineers, Car Mechanics, Florists, Refuse Collectors, Publicans and Newsagents.

It is not in any way elitist, all are treated equally and it is very much a meritocracy.

The origins of Freemasonry are shrouded in mystery and no one can really say for sure exactly when it all started.

Some say that Freemasonry started at the time of the building of King Solomon's Temple in Jerusalem when something like 100,000 – 130,000 stone masons were employed in its construction.

At the time of its completion, King Solomon's Temple in Jerusalem was considered to be the greatest architectural structure ever built. The stone masons associated with its construction would likely to have been considered the crème de la crème of engineering expertise of the time.

It's not hard to imagine the stone masons of the time forming some sort of guild or trade association to protect the skills and knowledge that they had developed whilst working on such a project. Equally, recognition signals would have been introduced to demonstrate that they had actually worked on the construction project. When the Temple was finished, tens of thousands of stone masons would have dispersed around the then known world to work on other construction projects. Their skills and recognition signals would have been passed down from generation to generation over the centuries.

Consider the situation that the King of another country at the time wanted to build a cathedral or a castle. How would he have known that a stone mason or an architect at the time had the necessary skills and abilities to build something that wouldn't fall down after a couple of years? Nowadays, artisans have references that they could show to prospective employers. In biblical times, there would have been other ways of identifying skills and talents and these recognition signals would have been ideal.

Some say that King Athelstan of England in the 10th Century issued the first charter to a Masonic Lodge.

Whether this is true or not, the true origins of Freemasonry have been lost in the midst of time. However, there is without a doubt that medieval guilds of stone masons existed in the middles ages, just as the growth of other "professional" guilds developed in the middle ages – Grocers, Butchers, Barber Surgeons, Needle makers, Candle makers, Tanners, Furriers, Coopers, etc.

The inclusion of the word *"Free"* as part of *Free*masonry, is to emphasise that you had to be a *"Free"* man and not a slave in order to join.

In 1717, four Masonic lodges that had been meeting in London combined to form the first "Grand Lodge of England". They called themselves the Moderns. However, there had already been in existence another "Grand Lodge" – "The Ancient Grand Lodge of England". In 1813, both of these "Grand Lodges" –

the Moderns and Ancients, united to form The United

Grand Lodge of England which still exists today.

# Freemasonry and Religion

Freemasonry is not a religious organisation. In fact, the word "God" is hardly ever used in Masonic ritual. However, in order to join Freemasonry, a new member has to have a belief in a "Supreme Being". In other words, atheists cannot join Freemasonry. By having a non-specific Supreme Being enables believers of all and any faiths to become Freemasons – Christians, Catholics, Jews, Muslims, Sikhs, etc – provided that the individual believes in a Supreme Being.

At Masonic meetings, a holy book or bible is open at all times and candidates are asked to swear oaths of secrecy with their hand on the bible, just like a witness would do in Court. However, the candidate can choose whether the holy book is the Old

Testament, the New Testament, The Koran or any other religious book of their specific faith.

In Masonic ritual, the Supreme Being is referred to by various non-specific terms – for example, The Great Architect of The Universe, The Grand Geometrician of The Universe, The Almighty Friend of all Friends, The Most High, etc. This enables individuals of all faiths to give respect to their own Supreme Being without giving offence to individuals of other religions.

# What does it cost to join?

I believe there is a lot of misinformation about the cost of being a Mason.  I have heard it said that you have to be truly wealthy to join a lodge and then maintain membership.

Obviously, lodges are all different to one another. Nonetheless, in principal they are all run along the same general lines.  In fact, most of the costs of actually "running" the lodge are fixed.  There are **four** main costs associated with the financial management of a lodge.

The first two are the "per head dues/subscriptions" to UGLE and the local province in which the lodge is based.  These in themselves make up the bulk of the revenue that the lodge needs to raise in order to survive.

The third major cost is the rent needed to hire a room for the lodge meeting to be held. The fourth major cost is the cost of the meal after the actual lodge meeting.

Lodges that meet in London are usually more expensive than Lodges that meet in the provinces.

At the time of writing, I would estimate that a Lodge in the Provinces would charge an annual subscription of between £150 and £200 with the cost of the meal afterwards costing around £15 to £25.

This would make the annual cost of membership somewhere in the region of £200 - £300. Probably a lot less than most people imagine and certainly a lot less than other activities –for instance, playing golf, supporting your local premiership football club or going to the opera.

On top of that, there is a joining fee usually equivalent to the annual subscription plus a small cost for certain regalia – white gloves, Masonic tie and Masonic apron – probably around £50.

# What goes on at Masonic Meetings?

In general, Masonic meetings are divided into two parts.

One part concerns the general running and management of an organisational body, just like any committee or society.

There will be minutes of previous meetings and a treasurers' report to discuss the financial aspects of the lodge, fees and subscriptions, etc.

On top of that, there will usually be an almoner's report. Most lodges have an almoner and his role is to look after and liaise with widows of former members as well as members who are struggling with health issues. In many cases, the almoner will visit to try and offer assistance to such widows and members in any way that he feels able to assist.

There will usually be a report by the Charity Steward. Prior to the introduction of the national lottery in the UK, Freemasonry was the largest body making charitable donations. Quite literally, many millions of pounds are donated by Masonic lodges to charitable bodies, which include the air ambulance services, guide dogs for the blind, RNLI, cancer research, etc.

Even today, Freemasonry is considered to be one of the largest organisation making charitable donations, along with the national lottery, Help for Heroes and the BBC's Children in Need.

In general, UGLE and the Masonic provincial bodies support major charitable bodies and the local lodges support smaller community based charities.

For example, in my London Lodge, we raised enough money to train a guide dog. Another lodge raised money specifically to purchase a specialist child's bed for a local children's hospice. Another province raised money to provide a defibrillator in every ambulance in the county.

Another province raised money so that every child admitted to hospital in their county could be given a teddy bear.

In one of the villages near where I live, a little girl was killed in a road accident. The parents wanted to have a bench put in the local park to commemorate their daughter's life. The local lodge contributed £150 towards the purchase of the bench.

The charity collection is made at the end of most lodge meetings. Each member is asked to contribute whatever they each feel comfortable in giving. No one knows what other members put in the collection box – whether it is 50p, £5 or £50 – it all goes to charity.

Having considered the general running and management of the lodge, the second major part of the lodge meeting concerns what Masons call "The Ritual".

In essence, this is the actual ceremony that Masons go through to join and then progress through the lodge.

I should emphasise that there is nothing in the ritual designed to embarrass or humiliate a candidate. Nothing can be further from the truth.

There are three stages of progression through a Masonic lodge and for the ease of reference I will call them the first, second and third degrees.

I am told there are up to 33 degrees but I've never come across anyone who has actually done that many. I would guess that you'd have to give up virtually all your leisure time to get involved in so many lodge meetings that, to me, it would be like having a full time job. However, if that's what some people want to do, that's fine if they want to do it, but it's not for me.

In fact, the three ceremonies that a new member goes through will be virtually identical to the three ceremonies that all existing and current members experienced when they themselves first joined Freemasonry. They are certainly identical to the ceremonies that I experienced when I first joined Freemasonry thirty five years ago.

What actually happens in the lodge ceremony is a bit complicated to explain but here goes.

Each Lodge will have a Master – the Worshipful Master as he is called. He is the most senior person in the lodge for that year.

He leads the ceremony involving new members.

In addition to the Worshipful Master, there are usually 5 other officers who take part in the ritual. If we assume that the Worshipful Master is in office no. 1, then we could call the next most senior member of the lodge officer no. 2, the next most senior member after that would be officer no. 3, and so on through the lodge until we come to officer no. 6.

What actually happens in the lodge is similar in principal to a small one act play. Imagine a play by Shakespeare with this major difference. The candidate himself [i.e. the person who is actually joining the lodge] is actually the star of the show.

However, I'm sure that it hasn't escaped your notice that the candidate himself hasn't got a clue what's going on.  He doesn't know where to stand, what to say, where to go, etc.

To facilitate the actual ceremony, one of the lodge officers will metaphorically hold his hand throughout the ceremony.  The lodge officer will tell the candidate what to say, when to say it, where to go and where to stand throughout the whole ceremony.  At no time is the candidate left on his own and there is always someone whispering in the candidate's ear telling him what to do.

The same goes for each of the three ceremonies – hence the expression "giving someone the three degrees".

Lodges meet on the same days each month each year. So for example, a lodge might meet on the third

Tuesday in February, the second Wednesday in April, the fourth Tuesday in October and the second Tuesday in December.

These dates are agreed when the lodge is first formed and one of these dates is selected as being the date when the new master is installed.  This meeting then becomes known as The Installation Meeting and the lodge year runs from one Installation Meeting to the next.  So, for example, if the Installation Meeting is held on the second Tuesday in December of one year until the second Tuesday in December of the following year, that period between the two Installation Meetings is known as the lodge year.

At the end of the lodge year, the Worshipful Master vacates the Master's chair and becomes what is known as The Immediate Past Master [the IPM]. The IPM then installs officer no. 2 as the new Worshipful Master.

Each officer then moves up one office.  So officer no. 3 becomes the new officer no. 2.  Officer no. 4 becomes the new officer no. 3 and so on.  The most senior of the lodge members who has not already held an office becomes the new officer no. 6.

After, say, two or three years, the newly joined member would have sufficient experience to take his role as officer no. 6 when it becomes available.

By this simple officer progression, each officer in the lodge takes a turn at each role within the lodge. This means that by the time he becomes the Worshipful Master, he has taken his turn at each level of officer.

# Other Masonic Orders

The basic unit of Freemasonry is the Masonic Lodge, which alone can initiate a Freemason. Such lodges are controlled by UGLE. Once you have completed your Third Degree and become what is known as a master mason, a whole panoply of other orders open up to you.

Amongst these, you will find The Holy Royal Arch, The Order of Mark Master Masons, the Order of the Secret Monitor, Rose Croix, Knights Templar, The Order of Royal and Select Masters, The Order of the Red Cross of Constantine, Allied Masonic Degrees, The Order of the Scarlet Cord, The Order of Knight Masons, The Royal Order of Scotland, The Ancient and Accepted Scottish Rite, The Masonic Knights Templar, Order of Royal Ark Mariners, plus many more.

Each of these orders have their own ritual, regalia and "secrets". There is absolutely no obligation to join any other orders. Generally, if you are the sort of person who enjoys Masonic meetings, enjoys meeting with like-minded people and enjoys the atmosphere of the ritual, you might well be someone who wants to join other orders and degrees, but it is entirely voluntary.

As mentioned earlier, I originally joined a London Lodge. I now live on the Oxfordshire/ Buckinghamshire border. I am a member of lodges and orders that meet in Thame, Beaconsfield, Wallingford, Aylesbury and Cambridge. Over the years I have been a guest at lodge meetings in St. Albans, Northampton, Redditch, Marlow, Slough, Winslow, Bletchley, Olney, Wokingham, Sindlesham, Southgate, Witney, Burford and Stow-on-the Wold.

Why have I joined lodges in different locations and visit other lodges? Well, there are two reasons.

Firstly, I enjoy it and, secondly, I get to meet and enjoy the company of other professional people.

# Lodge of Instruction

Most Lodges have a Lodge of Instruction, known as the LOI.

The LOI is a regular meeting of the lodge members where the officers are effectively taught how to perform the ritual. Just like a Shakespearean play, the officers have to learn words off by heart and the LOI is the environment where that happens.

Each lodge member is given a small black ritual book which has all the words he needs to learn as he progresses through the lodge.

Each year the lodge appoints a "Preceptor" whose role it is to teach the junior members of the lodge how to perform the ritual of the three degrees.

The LOI is also a great way for the individual lodge members to get to know each other socially and many LOIs finish up in the pub afterwards.

Most LOIs take place during the winter months of the year and happen once every week or every other week depending on how many lodge meetings there are.  Most LOIs last no more than ninety minutes.

# The Festive Board

The festive board is essentially the meal that follows the lodge meeting.

As most lodges meet in the evening, the festive board is usually a dinner.  Having said that, one of the lodges that I'm a member of meets on a Saturday morning and so the festive board is a lunch.

Most provincial lodge meetings start during the late afternoon, say 17:00 or 18:00.

The actual lodge meeting lasts approximately one and a half hours and so will finish around 19:30. There will be short interval for pre-dinner drinks, the meal will start at around 20:00 and finish around 22:00.

London lodge meetings usually start and finish earlier as many of the brethren [i.e. the lodge members] could have up to a two hour journey to get home. In the provinces, most brethren live within a thirty minute drive.

When I first joined Freemasonry, copious amounts of wine were consumed. However, with the poor public transport in the provinces and the introduction of stringent drink-driving legislation, most lodge members drink much less than they used to, but wine is still available as well as shandy, fruit juice, ginger beer, cola or lemonade.

During the meal, a toast will be drunk to The Queen, the Grand Master [currently H R H The Duke of Kent], other Grand Officers and Masonic dignitaries.

The IPM will invariably say a few polite words about the Worshipful Master and propose a toast to him.

Then, the Worshipful Master will follow this by spending a few minutes responding to that toast.

If there is a new member joining the lodge, there will also be toast "to the initiate" and he in turn will say few words in response.

Many lodge members will invite guests to both the lodge meeting and the festive board.  At some meetings I've been to, the guests can make up more than half of those present.

A toast is usually made to the visitors and one of the guests will be asked to respond on behalf of all the visitors.

In most lodges, there is a raffle.  Invariably, the Worshipful Master will provide a one litre bottle of whiskey or equivalent as the top prize and other brethren will donate other prizes – bottles of wine, boxes of chocolate, etc. The raffle costs are usually £5 for five tickets with all the funds taken going to charity.

The festive board invariably ends with what is known as "The Tyler's Toast" which is essentially a toast "to all poor and distressed freemasons".

There are a couple of subjects that are completely forbidden at lodge meetings and the subsequent festive boards.

In general, any subjects that are or could be considered controversial are avoided – foremost amongst these are politics and religion. In some cases, I've even heard disapproving comments where someone talked about their favourite football team and how they had beaten their local rival. In general, the Masonic environment is meant to be one of peace and harmony and anything that could lead to disagreements are avoided.

Promoting one's business is also not allowed. The festive board is very much a social interaction. There is no agenda and apart from promoting one's business or anything contentious, people talk about whatever subjects that want to talk about – family, holidays, the TV, the Olympics, films – whatever they like.

Some years ago I was invited to what is known as a "White Table" event.

A "White Table" is usually a function where non Masons as well as the wives and girlfriends of masons are invited to a social event. It is also an occasion where potential joiners come along to meet and socialise with Masons, especially if they are considering joining.

At one such an event, one of the guests stood up and announced to everyone at his dining table that he provided personal financial advice and that if anyone required investment advice, a pension plan or an insurance policy, he was the man to see.

I can 100% guarantee that not only would he NOT be invited to another White Table, but that he had a 0% chance of ever being invited to join a lodge.

# Negative views of Freemasonry

It cannot be denied that there are many negative views held of Freemasonry.  In general, these views are invariably one of jealousy, ignorance or intolerance.

I have heard views that Freemasons run the country, control the Police and are even in charge of the Judiciary.

I'm sure there are many Freemasons who hold high and influential offices in the country.  However, for every one of those, there are probably hundreds of plumbers, milkmen, postmen, newsagents, etc who just enjoy Freemasonry just for the pleasure it gives them.

Some years ago, there was some negative publicity because two Masons met at a Masonic meeting and then they conspired to rob a bank.

Freemasonry seemed to have got the blame.

However, if these same two men had met at, say, a golf club, a chess club or a church meeting, I doubt if anyone would have suggested we ban chess, golf or going to church.

## Masonic Secrets

Much is made of the so called Masonic secrets. Many people would describe Freemasonry as a secret society.

I take a different view and describe it as a society that has secrets.

This might have been true in the past, but now the so called Masonic secrets can easily be discovered within a 5 minute search on the internet. Some people refer to strange handshakes and rolled up trouser legs as if this is somehow going to lead them to a seat on the board of a PLC or an important role in Government.

As a simple analogy, consider what actually happens at a company's board meeting. The Directors will discuss certain future actions that the company may or may not follow.  However, the minutes taken at the meeting are only circulated to the Directors.  Those minutes and the discussions that took place are just as much a secret as what goes on at lodge meetings.

Would anyone honestly think that board meetings of Directors constitute some sort of secret society? Quite simply, if you want to find out what happens at board meetings, then become a director.  Equally, if you want to find out what happens at Masonic meetings, then join a lodge.

From a personal perspective, when I first became a Company Director, I was incredibly disappointed in the actual experience of attending board meetings. To my dismay, I also found that whatever information I discovered, I was duty bound to keep confidential from the rest of the company's employees.

However, if you really want to find out about the so called Masonic secrets, then I can do little more than recommend a visit to the UGLE offices in Great Queen Street, Holborn.

There you will find a museum full of Masonic literature and history. It is completely free and open to the public.

However, just like most churches and cathedrals, a small donation is requested to assist in the maintenance of the building.

For a tour of Freemasons Hall in Holborn, take a look at: www.ugle.org.uk/freemasons-hall/tours and www.freemasonry.london.museum/tours

A number of governments, especially totalitarian or one party states, have treated Freemasonry as a potential source of opposition due to its so called secret nature and international connections.

The Nazis claimed that high-degree Masons were willing members of the Jewish conspiracy and that Freemasonry was one of the causes of Germany's defeat in World War. In Mein Kampf, Adolf Hitler wrote that Freemasonry had succumbed to the Jews and had become an excellent instrument to fight for their aims and to use their strings to pull the upper strata of society into their designs. In 1933 Hermann Göring, the Reichstag President and one of the key figures in the process of Gleichschaltung ("synchronization"), stated "in National Socialist Germany, there is no place for Freemasonry".

During the war, Freemasonry was banned by edict in all countries that were either allied with the Nazis or under Nazi control, including Norway and France.

Anti-Masonic exhibitions were held in many occupied countries.

As the Nazis conquered Europe, the Germans forcibly dissolved Masonic organizations and confiscated their assets and documents wherever they established an occupation regime. After a lodge was closed, it was ransacked for membership lists, important library and archival items, furnishings and other cultural artefacts.

However, in the time between the two world wars, it was quite common for local newspapers to carry adverts announcing that "Butcher Joe Blow would be join the XYZ lodge on such a date and that other masons would be welcome to attend the meeting".

There were even public processions of Freemasons through the streets of London wearing their aprons, collars, insignias and jewels.

As the Nazis occupied more and more of Europe, UGLE took the view to move Freemasonry "underground". When UGLE saw what the Nazis were doing to Freemasons in the Channel Islands after their occupation and with the fear of a possible invasion into the UK mainland, Freemasons became virtually invisible to the general public and the myth of Masonic secrets started to spread.

# How to Join

Anyone offering himself as a candidate should be 21 years of age or over, of good repute and should be entirely assured in his own mind:

1. that he sincerely seeks intellectual and moral improvement for himself and others.

2. that he has a belief in a supreme being (God as you understand him).

3. that he is able to afford the necessary expenditure without detriment to himself or his connections. Financial ability to pay lodge subscriptions and contribute to charity, without having an adverse impact on his family.

4. that he is willing and able to devote part of his time, his means and his efforts, to the promotion of the

aims of our ancient Institution. To make a commitment to attend Lodge meetings, rehearsals, socials and events.

5. that he will never seek commercial, social or pecuniary advantage from his membership.

In the "olden days", it was generally believed that you had to be asked to join a lodge.  Nowadays, it is perfectly acceptable, indeed encouraged, to make contact with Freemasonry directly by expressing an interest in learning more and possibly joining a lodge. Of course, making an enquiry does not obligate you to join.

An application form can be found at

www.ugle.org.uk/contact-us/interested-in-joining/view/form

You will then be put in touch with a lodge that meets either close to where you work, where you live or where you study – depending on your preferences.

Someone from a local lodge will then arrange to meet you and probably take you to the local Masonic hall.

If you decide you wish to proceed with your application, that person will then invite another member of the lodge to meet you.

It is generally acknowledged that you will need both a proposer and a seconder to join a lodge and that both your proposer and seconder will have to have known you for a minimum of 6 months before you can formally apply to join a lodge.

During that six months period, you are likely to be invited to whatever social events that the lodge organises. This will give you an opportunity to meet other members of the lodge, socialise with them and make sure you feel comfortable in their company.

At the end of the six months, you will probably be invited to a formal interview by The Lodge Committee. The Lodge Committee invariably consists of the Worshipful Master, Past Masters and other senior officers of the Lodge.

This is not meant to be some sort of test of your Masonic knowledge but is just a friendly interaction between you and the senior members of the lodge. It's important that the lodge members get to know you just as much as you get to meet them. The lodge members will ask you questions. You in turn will have the opportunity to ask the lodge members questions about Freemasonry, what is expected of you in terms of financial commitment, time commitment, etc.

Most of these interviews will last between thirty and forty five minutes. You will then be asked to leave the room for a short time whilst the lodge members discuss your application for membership.

On the assumption that the lodge committee members support your application to join, the next step is for the full lodge members to be balloted on for your membership which will usually take place at the next lodge meeting after your interview.

As most lodges only meet four or five times during the year, there could be a considerable delay before you find out whether the ballot has been successful in your favour.

However, even at this stage, there is still no obligation for you to join. You could withdraw your application at any time or even defer it until a later date, especially if your financial, employment or domestic circumstances change.

On the assumption that the ballot has been successful in your favour, the lodge secretary will write to you and formally inform you. He will also give you one or two dates when the lodge would be able to perform the ceremony of your initiation.

Don't be surprised if the whole process takes twelve or even eighteen months from the time you apply to the time you actually join.

Your proposer will tell you what to expect on the evening of your initiation.

With regard to what to wear, I would suggest you dress as though you had an interview with a bank manager or for a job interview – black or dark blue suit, plain white shirt, black or dark blue socks, black tie and black shoes.

You will be expected to buy a pair of white gloves and also a plain black tie, the sort you'd wear at a funeral. Some lodges have their own tie which you will be expected to buy at some point in time.

You have probably heard that freemasons wear Masonic aprons. You do not need to worry about an apron as one will be provided for you at the meeting.

You should also be prepared to say a few words of thanks to your proposer and seconder at the festive board for inviting you to join the lodge. When I say "a few words", I really mean that – you should be prepared to talk for no more than a minute.

# So what is expected of you as a Mason?

There is no definitive list. However, at the very least, I would suggest:

That you accept that there is such a thing as honour and that a man has a responsibility to act with honour in everything he does.  That a life NOT founded on honour is hollow and empty.

That you believe in a Supreme being.

That you are willing to allow others to the same right to their own beliefs in religious, social and political matters that you insist on yourself.

To tolerate that other people have the right to think for themselves and hold their own opinions in religious, social and political matters.

That you have a belief that you have a responsibility to leave the world a better place than you found it.

That you have a duty not only to yourself but to others. You must do what you can to make the world a better place.

That it is not only more blessed to give than it is to receive, but that usually it's also more fun.

Much of the help we give others is given anonymously. We're not after gratitude.

Are you willing to give your brothers help when they need it and likewise accept it when you in turn need it? Not financial help, but help in the sense of being there when needed, giving support and lending a sympathetic ear.

That you feel there is more to life than purely financial success.

That you recognise that social development is a key part to our lives – sometimes more important than money in the bank, social status or political power.

That you should strive to be a good citizen. That you have a moral duty to be true to the country in which you live and to honour and respect the laws and culture of that country.

That you should show compassion to those less fortunate than ourselves.

# A final word

I have been a Freemason for as long as I can remember. I was a mason before I met my wife and long before my children were born.

Although I have many interests outside of Freemasonry, I can honestly say that by far the majority of my closest friends are those that I have met through Freemasonry.

In the UK there are around 250,000 masons and around 8,000 active lodges.

There is no higher accolade to Freemasonry that I can add other than to say that I have held it in such high esteem that I even encouraged my own father to join – and he got tremendous pleasure and satisfaction from it, especially as he got older.

Feel free to contact me with any questions that you might have about Freemasonry by email via raymondafox@aim.com

If you want to know more about Freemasonry in England and Wales or join a Lodge in London or in the Provinces, go to:

www.ugle.org.uk/about/provinces

For Freemasonry in Scotland, go to:

www.grandlodgescotland.com

For Freemasonry in Ireland, go to:

http://freemason.ie

For information on Freemasonry for Women, go to:

www.owf.org.uk

29327388R00047

Printed in Great Britain
by Amazon